BRAIN QUEST

LEARN to WRITE

NUMBERS

T0015684

workman
• New York •

This book belongs to:

First Name

Last Name

ISBN 978-1-5235-1601-8

Design by Daniella Graner and John Passineau
Illustrations by Sean Sims
Edited by Alisha Zucker

Workman books are available at special discounts when purchased in bulk for premiums and sales promotions as well as for fundraising or educational use. Special editions or book excerpts can also be created to specification. For details, please contact special.markets@hbgusa.com.

Workman Publishing Co., Inc., a subsidiary of Hachette Book Group, Inc.
1290 Avenue of the Americas
New York, NY 10104

workman.com

Distributed in Europe by Hachette Livre, 58 rue Jean Bleuzen, 92 178 Vanves Cedex, France.

Distributed in the United Kingdom by Hachette Book Group, UK, Carmelite House, 50 Victoria Embankment, London EC4Y 0DZ.

Printed in Canada on responsibly sourced paper.

First printing July 2023

10 9 8 7 6 5 4 3 2 1

DEAR PARENTS AND CAREGIVERS,

At Brain Quest we believe learning is an adventure, a quest for knowledge. We're delighted to partner with you and your child as they begin their exciting journey exploring the fundamentals of writing.

LEARN TO WRITE: NUMBERS provides lots of opportunities for your child to practice writing numbers 0 through 20 and learn early math skills such as counting and understanding quantity. These skills build a foundation for more advanced math and set your child up for future math success.

Tips for Using This Book:

Follow your child's lead. Let them decide how much writing to do in one sitting.

Be hands on. Guide your child to trace the teal example numbers with their fingers and the light blue numbers with their pencils.

Offer support. Read the directions aloud. Model how to hold the pencil correctly as needed.

Praise their effort. Compliment your learner's effort and persistence.

Celebrate success! Use stickers from the back of the book to reward effort and success, and cut out the certificate to mark your child's accomplishment.

Enjoy this first step as your child learns to write!

—The editors of Brain Quest

Hold the pencil with the thumb and index fingers. Rest the pencil on the middle finger.

1

0 clouds

Trace the number **0**. Start at the **red** dot.

zero

Write the number **0**. Start at the **red dot**.

Circle the nests with **0** birds.

1

1 skyscraper

Trace the number **1**. Start at the **red** dot.

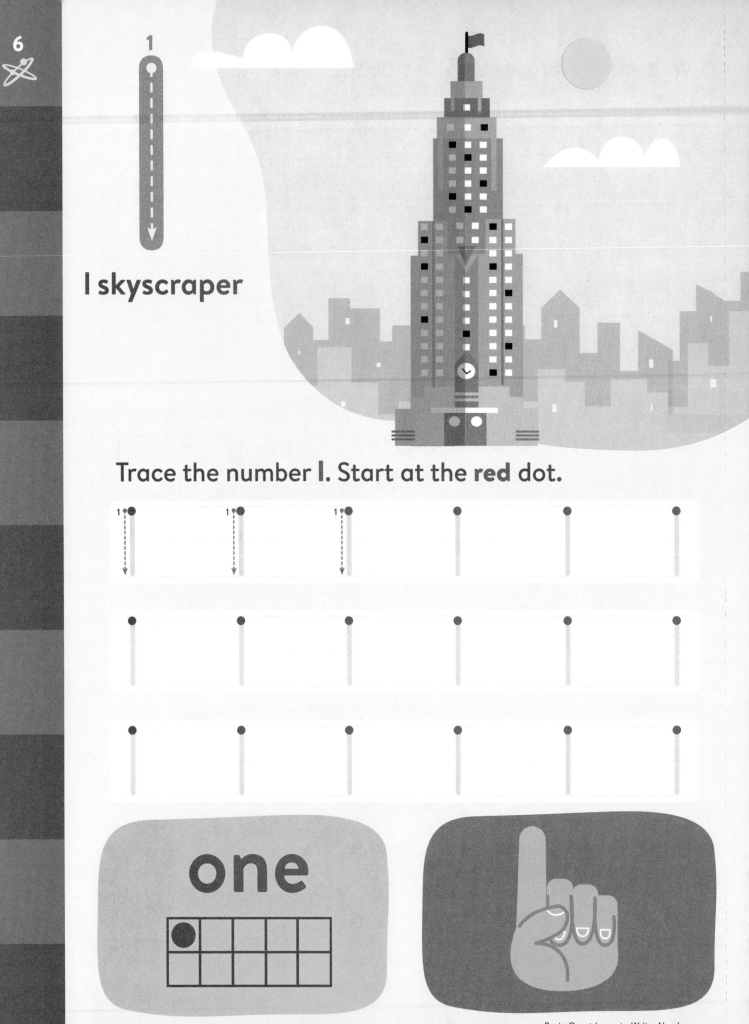

one

Write the number I. Start at the **red** dot.

Circle the Is.

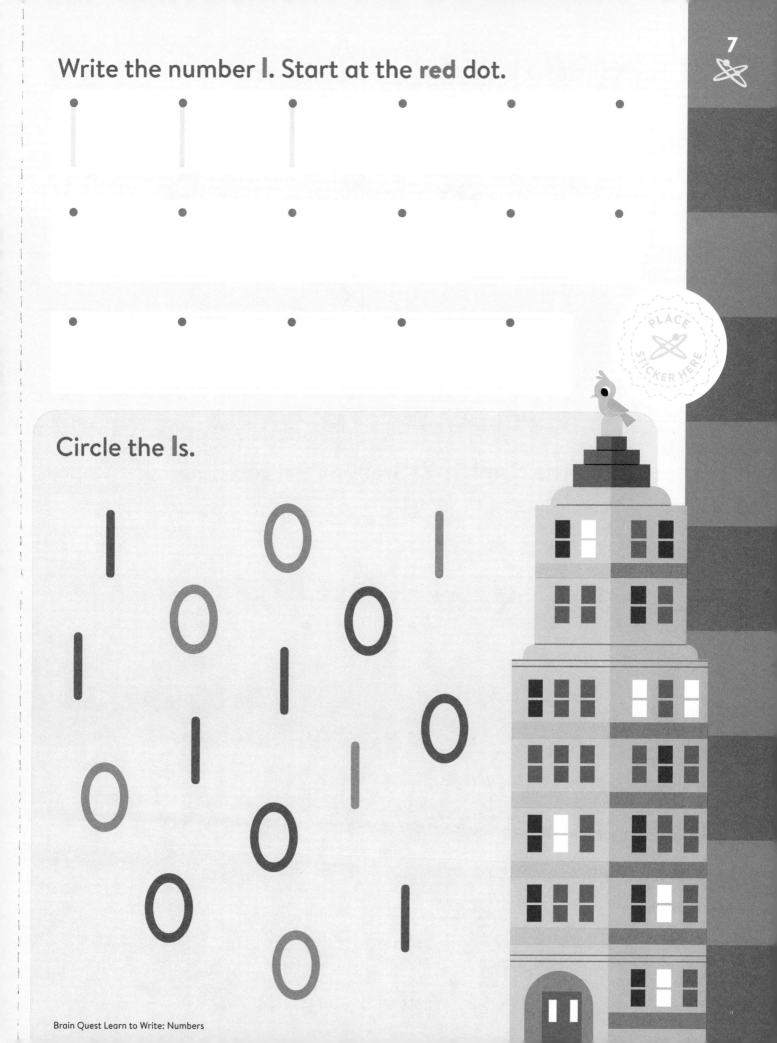

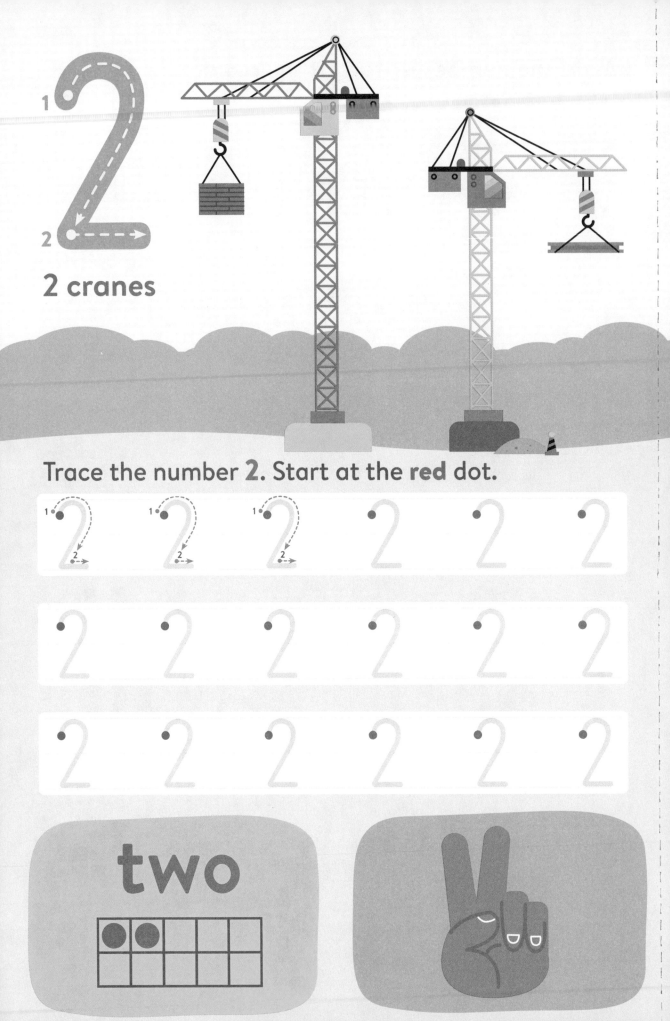

2 cranes

Trace the number **2**. Start at the **red** dot.

two

Write the number **2**. Start at the **red** dot.

2 2 2 • • •

• • • • • •

• • • • • •

Count the bulldozers.
Write the number in the box.

Let's Review

Count the dots on the dice.
Trace the number below.

2   0   1

Count the trucks. Trace each number.

0

1

2

Draw clouds in the sky to match the numbers.

Count the forklifts. Write the number in the box.

3 workers

Trace the number **3**. Start at the **red** dot.

three

Write the number **3**. Start at the **red** dot.

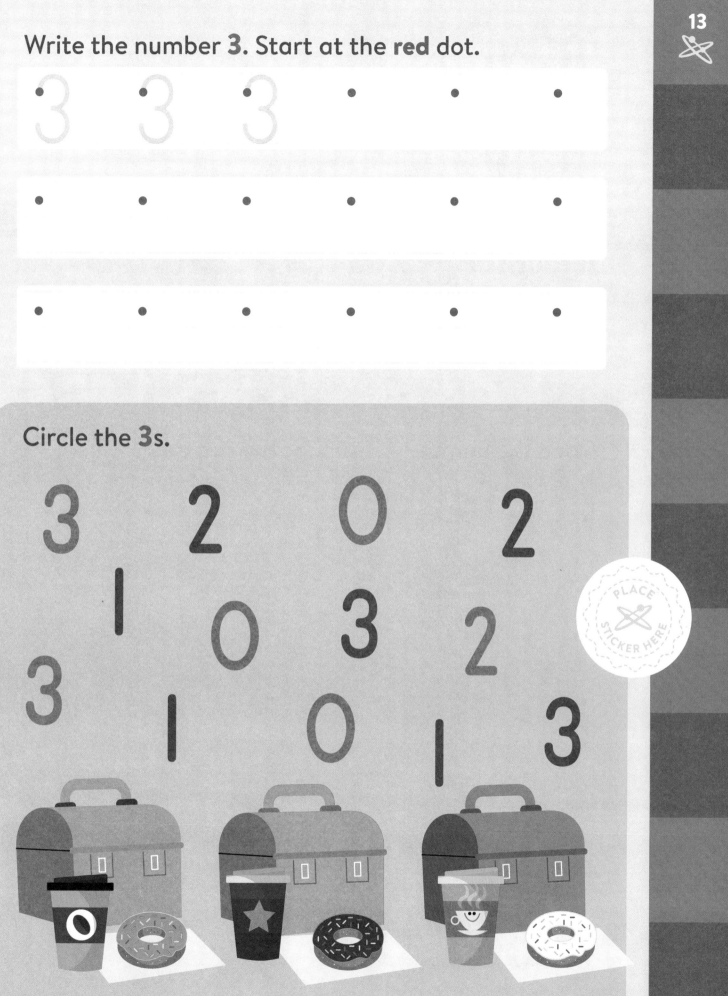

3 3 3 · · ·

· · · · ·

· · · · ·

Circle the **3**s.

3 2 0 2

1

0 3 2

3

1 0 1 3

4 tourists

Trace the number 4. Start at the **red** dot.

four

Write the number 4. Start at the **red** dot.

4 4 4

How many tour buses?
Write the number in the box.

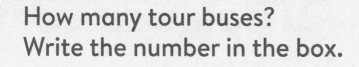

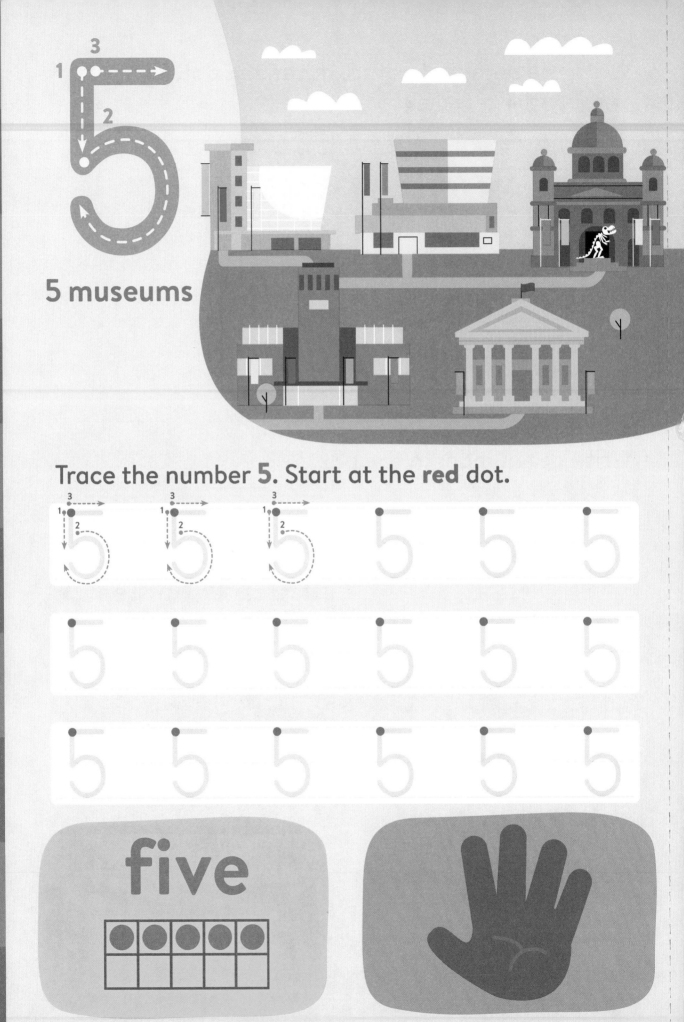

5 museums

Trace the number **5**. Start at the **red** dot.

five

Write the number 5. Start at the red dot.

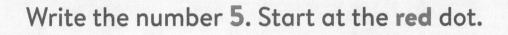

5　5　5

Circle the group of 5 dinosaurs.

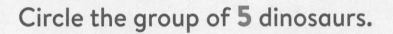

Let's Review

Count the dinosaurs.
Write the number in the box.

Color **3** of the paintings blue.

Color **5** of the paintings red.

6 ducks

Trace the number **6**. Start at the **red** dot.

six

Write the number 6. Start at the red dot.

6 6 6

Count the people on the bridge.
Write the number in the box.

7 skaters

Trace the number 7. Start at the red dot.

seven

Write the number 7. Start at the red dot.

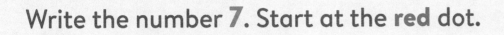

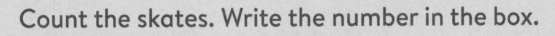

Count the skates. Write the number in the box.

8 cupcakes

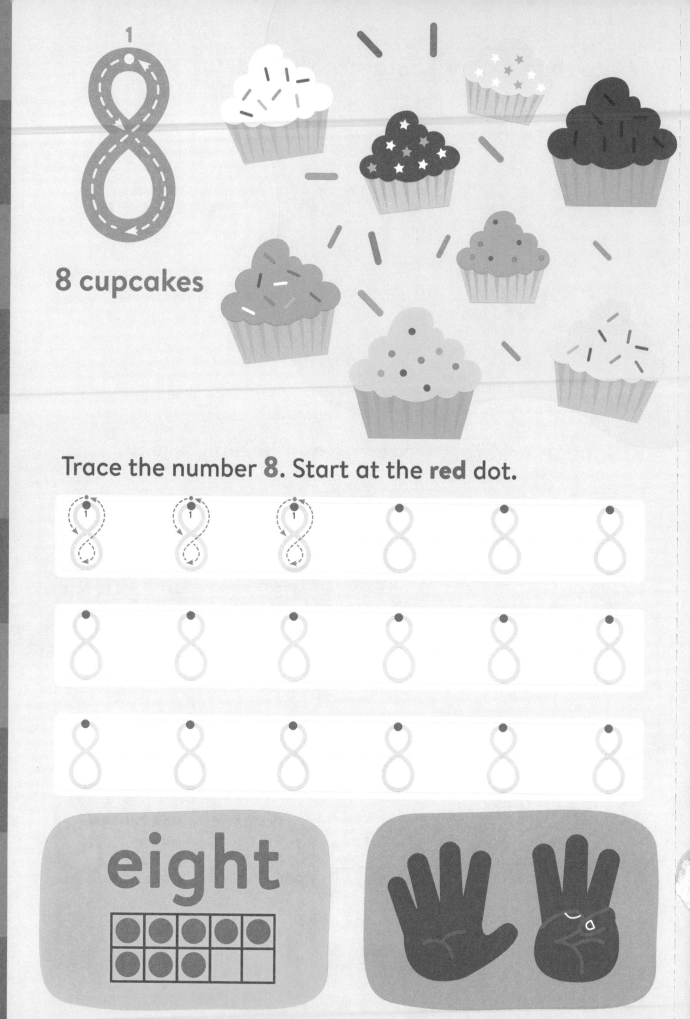

Trace the number **8**. Start at the **red** dot.

eight

Write the number 8. Start at the red dot.

888

Draw **8** candles on the cake.

HAPPY BIRTHDAY

PLACE STICKER HERE

Let's Review

Read the number on each cupcake.
Draw that number of sprinkles.

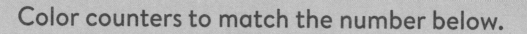

Color counters to match the number below.

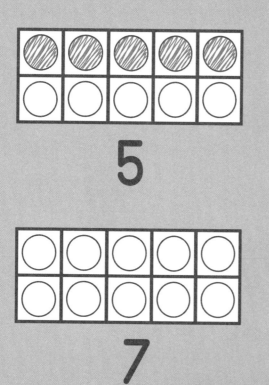

5

6

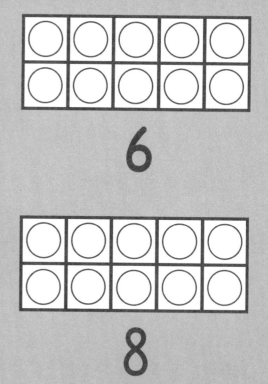

7

8

Trace the numbers. Then write the numbers below.

5   6   7   8

Count the swings. Write the number in the box.

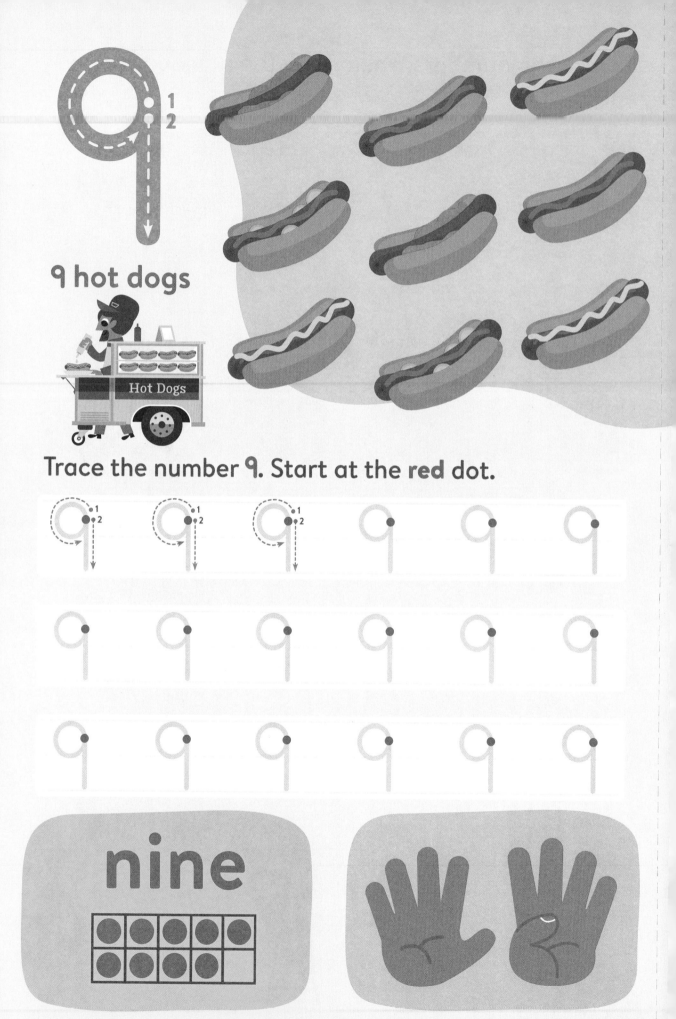

9 hot dogs

Trace the number 9. Start at the red dot.

nine

Write the number 9. Start at the red dot.

Count the pretzels. Write the number in the box.

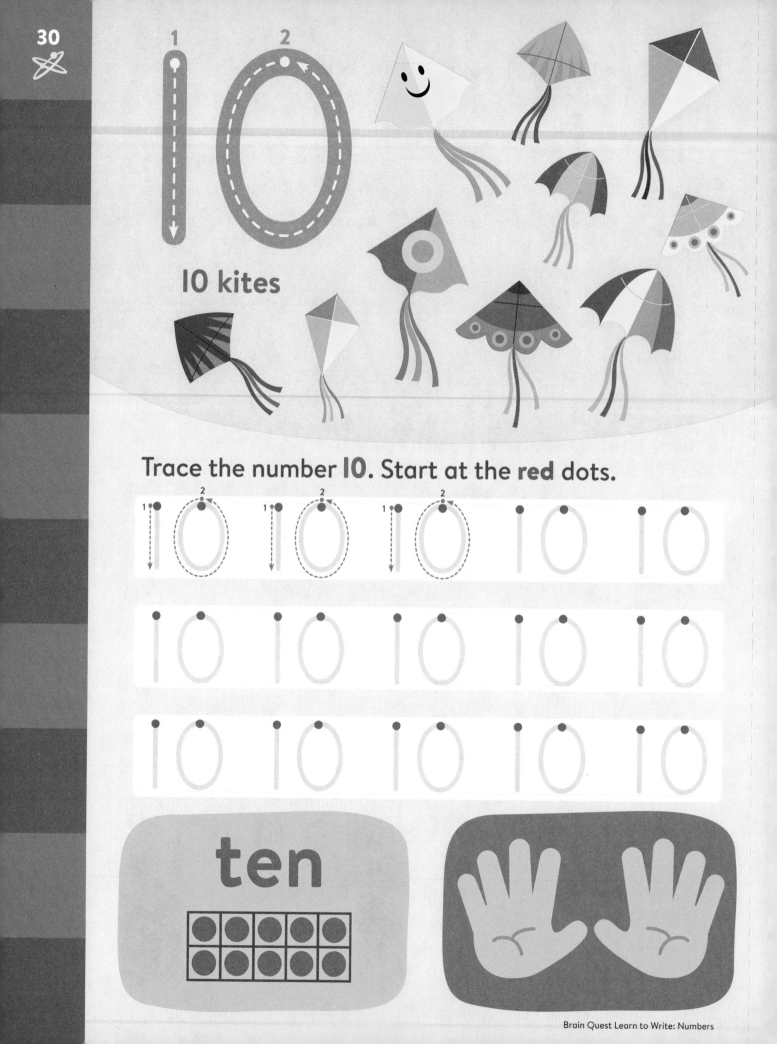

10

10 kites

Trace the number 10. Start at the red dots.

ten

Write the number **10**. Start at the **red dots**.

10 10 10

Draw **10** shapes on the kite.
Write the number in the box.

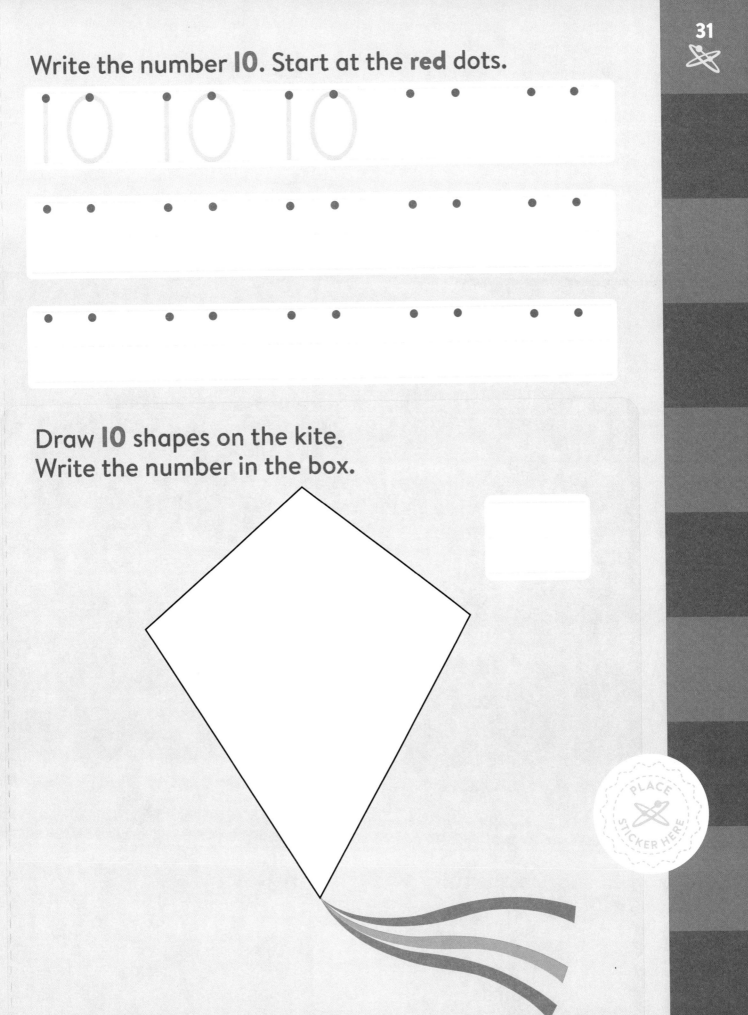

Let's Review

How many of each do you see?
Write the number in the box.

	squirrels		trees
	birds		people

Count from 0 to 10.
Write the missing numbers in the boxes.

0

[ ]

2

[ ]

4

5

[ ]

7

[ ]

[ ]

[ ]

11 balloons

Trace the number 11. Start at the **red** dots.

eleven

Write the number 11.
Start at the red dots.

Count the balloons.
Write the number in the box.

Hot Dogs

PLACE STICKER HERE

12

12 babies

Trace the number 12. Start at the red dots.

twelve

Write the number 12. Start at the red dots.

1 2 1 2 1 2

Circle the 12s.

10   12   1
12   10
  12   11
    12
1
      12
  11   2
2
  12

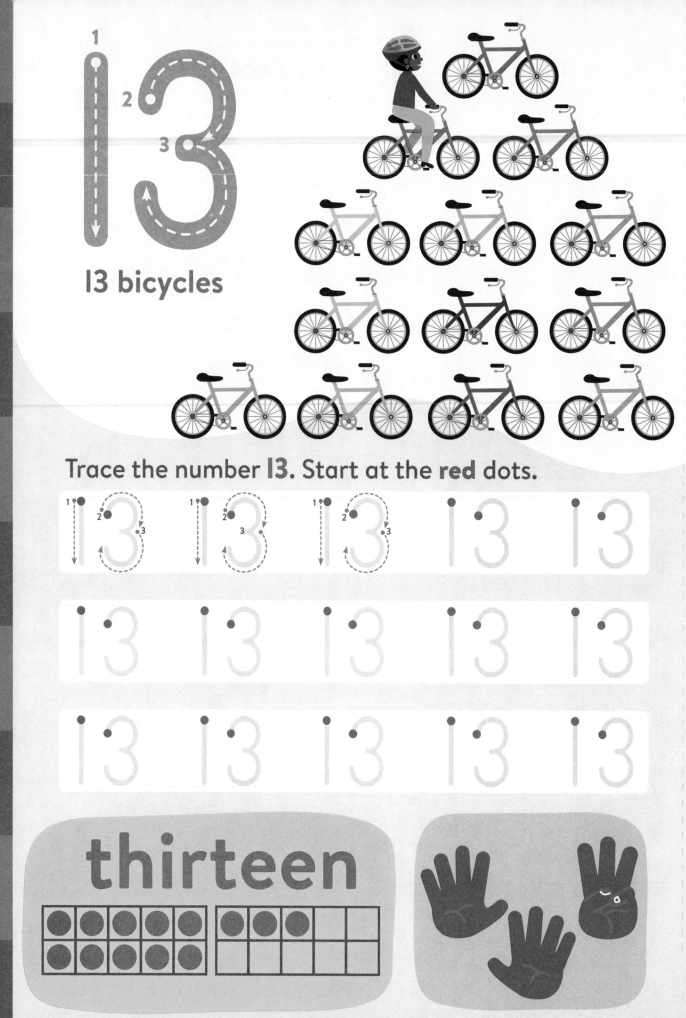

13 bicycles

Trace the number **13**. Start at the **red dots**.

thirteen

Write the number 13. Start at the red dots.

13 13 13

There are 13 helmets. Write the missing numbers.

1 2 ▢ 4

5 6 ▢ 8 9

10 ▢ 12 ▢

Let's Review

Draw a line from the numbers to the matching ten frames.

10

8

13

11

How many of each do you see?
Write the number in the box.

balloons

people

hot dogs

Hot Dogs

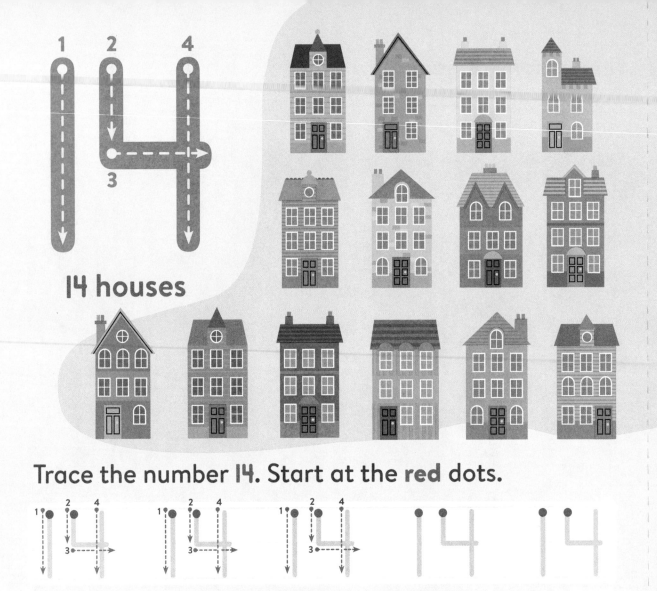

14 houses

Trace the number 14. Start at the **red** dots.

fourteen

Write the number 14. Start at the red dots.

14 14 14

How many birds on the birdhouse?
Write the number
in the box.

15 cones

Trace the number **15**. Start at the **red dots.**

fifteen

Write the number **15**. Start at the **red** dots.

15 15 15

Count the frozen treats on the menu.
Write the number in the box.

PLACE STICKER HERE

menu

Let's Review

Count the pictures.
Color the counters to show how many.

Count from **0** to **15**.
Write the missing numbers in the boxes.

0

1

3

5

7

9

11

13

16

16 boats

Trace the number 16. Start at the red dots.

1 2   1 2   1 2
16 16 16 16 16

16 16 16 16 16

16 16 16 16 16

sixteen

Write the number 16. Start at the red dots.

16 16 16

Color 16 fish. Write 16 in the box.

PLACE STICKER HERE

1 2 3

17 dogs

Trace the number **17**. Start at the **red dots**.

seventeen

Write the number 17. Start at the red dots.

17 17 17

How many dog bones do you count?
Write the number in the box.

18 pigeons

Trace the number **18**. Start at the **red dots.**

eighteen

Write the number **18**. Start at the **red dots**.

18   18   18

Count the pigeon feathers.
Write the number in the box.

Let's Review

dogs

houses

bikes

trucks

How many of each do you see?
Write the number in the box.

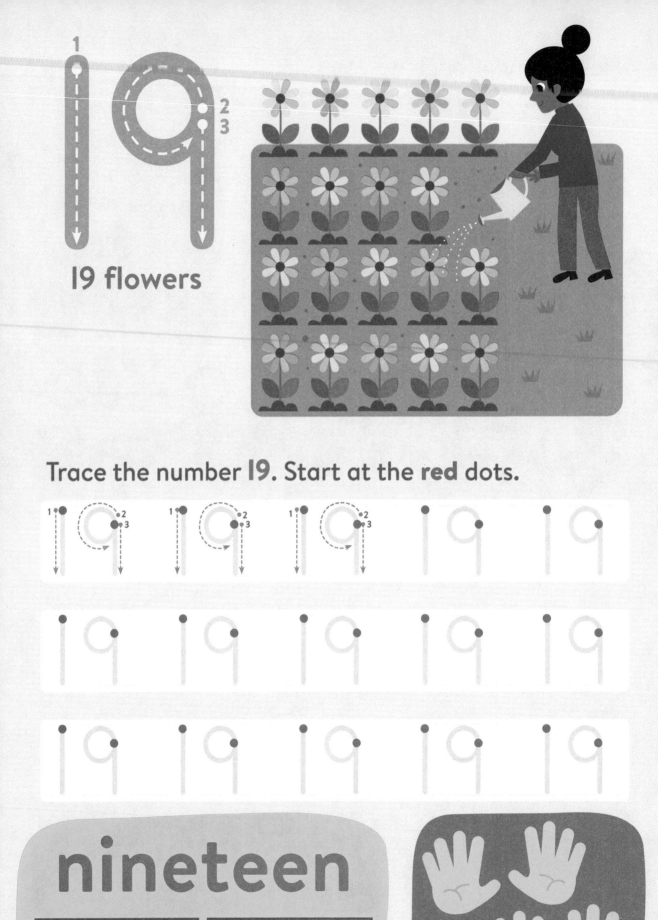

19 flowers

Trace the number 19. Start at the red dots.

nineteen

Write the number 19. Start at the red dots.

19   19   19

How many butterflies do you count?
Write the number in the box.

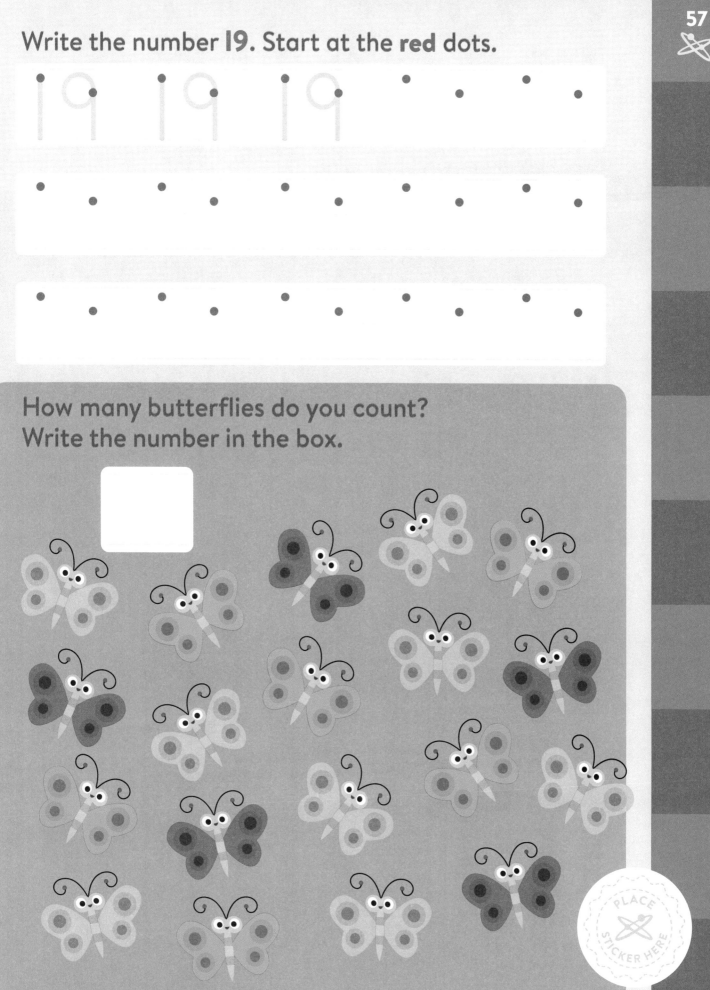

20

20 stars

Trace the number **20**. Start at the **red dots**.

twenty

Write the number **20**. Start at the **red** dots.

20 20 20

Count the fireworks. Write the number in the box.

Let's Review

Say each number aloud as you trace it.

Write the missing numbers.

Count and Color

How many of each do you see? Write the number in the box. Then color them all!

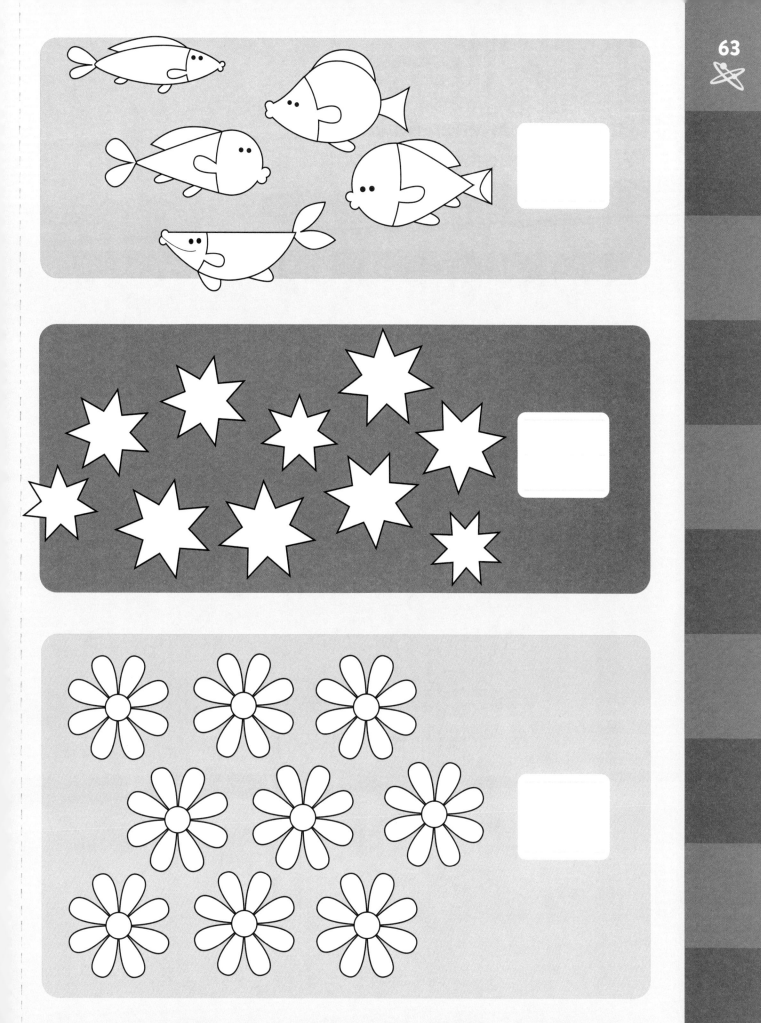

Toy Time!

How many of each do you see?
Write the number in the box.
Then color all the toys!

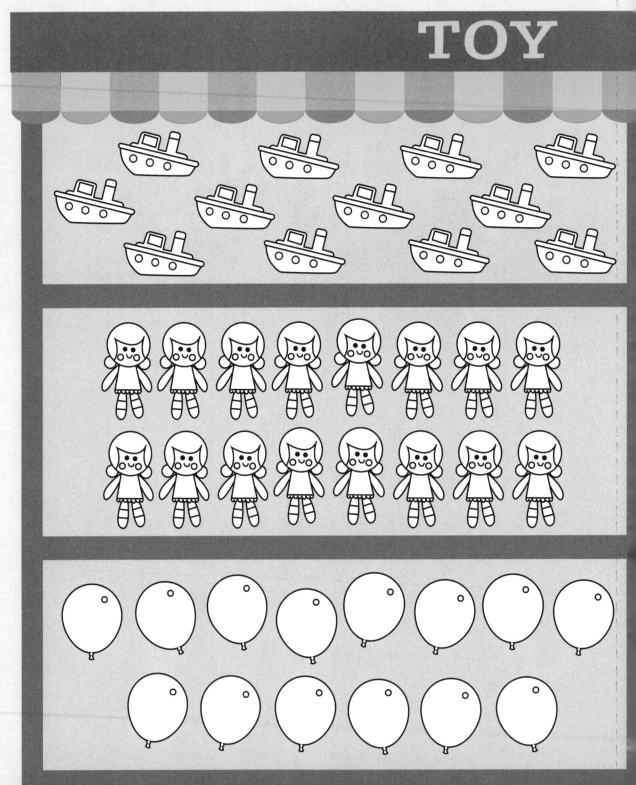

boats

dolls

balloons

balls

dinos

bears

SHOP

How Many?

How many of each do you see?
Write the number in the box.

Brain Quest Learn to Write: Numbers

Count It Out

Count out loud from 1 to 15.
Write the missing numbers in the boxes.

1 2 ☐ 4 5

6 7 8 ☐ 10

11 ☐ 13 ☐ 15

City Snacks

Count the pictures.
Color the counters to show how many.

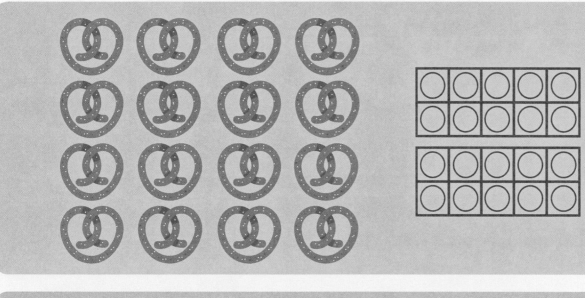

Count and Compare

Count the objects. Write how many in the boxes.
Circle the group that has more.

What's Missing?

Count out loud.
Write the missing numbers in the empty bus windows.

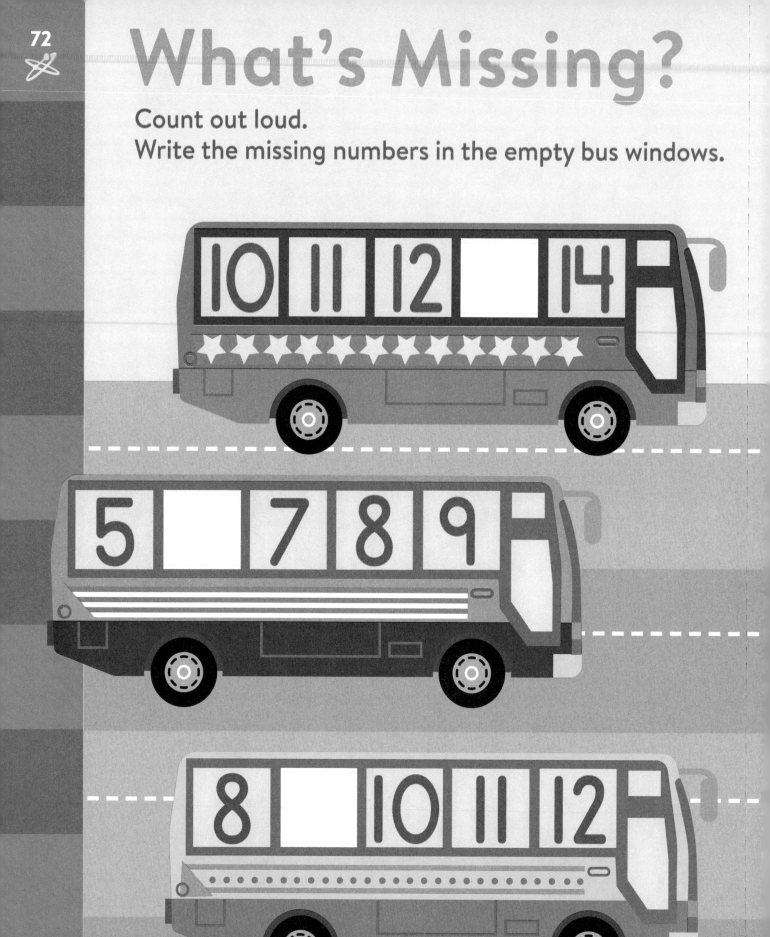

In the Middle

Write the missing number.

9 ☐ 11

18 ☐ 20

5 ☐ 7

13 ☐ 15

What Comes Next?

Say the first number out loud.
Count on and write the numbers that come next.

| 3 | 4 | 5 | 6 |

| 9 | | | |

| 11 | | | |

| 14 | | | |

Draw 20!

Draw 20 of your favorite things!
Write 20 in the box below.

All About Me

Write numbers to answer these questions.

How old are you?

I am [ ] years old.

What is your favorite number?

My favorite number is [ ].

How many pets do you have?

I have [ ] pets.

How many siblings do you have?

I have [ ] siblings.

How many people are in your family?

There are [ ] people in my family.

Draw your family here.

Matching

Trace the numbers. Draw lines to match the numbers to the fingers shown.

15

18

10

9

6

13

CONGRATULATIONS!

Write your name here:

COMPLETED

LEARN to WRITE NUMBERS

PLACE STICKER HERE

THERE'S MORE LEARN to WRITE

Practice tracing and writing lines, shapes, and letters with

More from America's #1 Educational Bestseller

BRAIN QUEST

Available wherever books are sold, or visit **brainquest.com.**

Trace the numbers and color the stickers!